EXPLORING
The Hāmākua Coast

HINODE   HONOMU   PEPEEK

EAST HAWAII JAP
JULY 26 1

EXPLORING

The Hāmākua Coast

Ken Okimoto

Watermark W Publishing

Design by Gonzalez Design Co.
Production by Randall Chun Design
Library of Congress Catalog Number: 00-00000
ISBN-10: 0-9720932-2-2
ISBN-13: 978-0-9720932-2-4

Exploring the Hāmākua Coast is an ongoing
community effort. Readers with additional information
about any of the photos or captions in this book
are invited to contact the publisher.

Watermark Publishing
1088 Bishop Street, Suite 310
Honolulu, HI 96813
Telephone: Toll-free 1-866-900-BOOK
Web site: www.bookshawaii.net
e-mail: sales@bookshawaii.net

Printed in the United States

Contents

Acknowledgments

The search for the photos in *Exploring the Hāmākua Coast* has been an unmarked and confusing trail through dusty basements, church archives, family albums on back porches, professional collections, business offices and unexpected sources. People have been very generous in their sharing, hospitality and enthusiasm. Their most consistent characteristic has been a pride in the history of their communities and a desire to share it with future generations.

Mahalo to Pastor Ron Kent of the Hilo Coast United Church of Christ, George and Tomiko Mine, Tsukasa and Kay Ishii, Tooru "Belly" and Helen Yugawa, Curtis Narimatsu and family, Pat Baptiste, the Pacific Tsunami Museum, Nani Pierce, the Lyman House Memorial Museum, Bishop Museum, the Laupahoehoe Train Museum, Lisa Barton, Leonie Kawaihona Poy, Sandra Gomes, Faye Honma, Thomas Nakahara family, Hal Hisa Yamato, the North Hawai'i Community Federal Credit Union, Gay Matthews, the Ikeuchi family, Paul Christensen, the Pāpa'ikou Hongwanji Mission, the Hawai'i State Archives, Ian Birnie, John O. May, Tadao Matsuzaki, the Pāpa'ikou Senior Citizens Club, Takashi Nonaka, Teruo Morigaki, the Martin family, Ayano Sadanaga, Wilbur Shigehara, Wallace Nagareda, Luika Perreira, Lizby Logsdon Ackerman, Bob Chow, Helen Wong Smith, Jack Roney, Haruko Hayashi, George Yokoyama and the Hawai'i County Economic Opportunity Council, Jessica Yamamoto and staff, Helen Shirota Benevides, the Kalaniana'ole School archives, Millie Kim, the Hawai'i Island Economic Development Board, Amy Iwamoto of the Hawai'i Electric Light Company, Aaron and Vinel Sugino, Rosita Cabatu, Rev. Daizo Watanabe, Shigeko Miyashiro, Waichi Ouye, Kepa Maly, Quentin Tomich, Peter Tomich, Jill Sommers, Paula Helfrich, Hiroshi Shima, Hideo Ishigo, Bob and June Asato, Minoru Hironaga, Haruko Hayashi and especially Tadao and Mitsue Okimoto. Sincere apologies if any sources have been omitted here.

A very special thank you to Hawai'i State Representative Dwight Takamine, the driving force behind *Exploring the Hāmākua Coast*.

Foreword

In the fall of 1994, after providing the economic base to an entire coastline of communities for more than a century, the last two sugar plantations along the Hilo-Hāmākua coastline closed their gates for good. While this marked the end of an era, it also provided for many new beginnings, and an opportunity to use the best from the past to help build an even better future.

This was our challenge, one that was met head-on by the many communities along the 50-mile coastline. Large or small, these communities pledged their cooperation from the start, heeding the rallying cry that "we are all in this together." Their response, which is still evolving, has been nothing less than inspirational.

I want to thank all of those individuals who helped to make *Exploring the Hāmākua Coast* a reality. This project reflects the rich heritage from many places that forms the strong foundation of a special people, a special history and a special story.

That story continues to unfold. This book, and the photos in these pages, will help make the story come alive, and lead us all to better understand the special values of the people who make up the communities along the Big Island's Hilo-Hāmākua coastline.

Dwight Takamine
State Representative
Hilo-Hāmākua District
The Big Island of Hawai'i

Introduction

Opinions differ on where the Hāmākua Coast actually begins and ends. Many on the Big Island of Hawaiʻi will tell you that it runs from Waipiʻo Valley in the north all the way down to the Wailuku River, gateway to the county seat of Hilo. Technically, only the northern third of this 40-mile shoreline falls in the Hāmākua District; the lower portion, in the Hilo District, is also known as the Hilo Coast. But over the years, this entire stretch has come to be known as the Hāmākua Coast, as indicated by the official state signs along Highway 19.

Whatever its parameters, the Hāmākua Coast is one of the most beautiful areas in the Hawaiian Islands, or anywhere. This spectacular slice of the tropics is a fertile crescent lying between the surging Pacific Ocean and the rolling foothills of the great volcano Mauna Kea. The Hāmākua Coast is a lush, picture-perfect place of rustic hamlets, hidden water-falls and wave-tossed bays. It is also one of Hawaiʻi's most historically significant areas, with roots in early Hawaiian civilization and the cultural diversity of the now-defunct sugar industry. *Exploring the Hāmākua Coast* offers both a look back at the area's rich history and a guide to help today's visitors discover its many natural and man-made attractions.

Whalers and Sugar Barons

It is believed that the Hāmākua Coast, like the rest of Hawaiʻi, was first inhabited by descendants of the ancient voyagers who sailed from the South Pacific, beginning some 1,500 years ago. Many of these early Hawaiians lived in numerous villages along the coast, amid a mixed-use landscape of forests, grasslands and cultivated farming areas.

In ancient Hawaiʻi, islands were divided into divisions, districts and various subdistricts called *ahupuaʻa*, shaped roughly like pie slices stretching from mountaintop to seashore. Such political boundaries encouraged fishermen, lowland farmers and upslope hunter-gatherers to share and trade with each other the bounties of their surroundings. Ocean fish were exchanged for lowland sweet potatoes or for wood products of the upper forests. Local leaders and commoners were the subjects of higher-ranking leaders, who in turn answered to those even higher in the sociopolitical hierarchy. Many factional battles were fought and alliances forged along the Hāmākua Coast.

In 1778 the British explorer Capt. James Cook "discovered" the Hawaiian Islands, and this European contact was soon followed by other explorers, whalers, missionaries and entrepreneurs. Whaling activity peaked in the mid-1800s, with Hilo Bay harboring many of the whalers, and declined in the years after the Civil War, as petroleum became more popular than whale oil for various uses.

Small sugar plantations were started along the coast and throughout the Hawaiian kingdom, and before long the island economy was dominated by the sugar industry and a plantation business elite with strong American ties. The industry received a big boost during the Civil War, when Hawaiʻi's product was much in demand to replace sugar suddenly unavailable from the Confederate states. Increased sugar production required the importing of labor, starting in the 1850s with workers from China, followed by immigrants from Japan in the 1860s, Portugal in the 1870s and the Philippines in the early 1900s. Smaller groups came from other lands: Korea, Puerto Rico, Scotland, Russia, Scandinavia and the U.S.

By the late 19th Century, several Hāmākua Coast sugar plantations were using narrow-gauge (tracks of three feet or less) railroads with portable tracks to transport harvested cane stalks out of the fields. Tracks were laid down to shoreline landings near the sugar mills for easier movement of cargo to freighters anchored offshore. By the early 1900s, a larger railway—the Hawaii Consolidated—was built to augment the old trails and small roads that followed the coast.

But competitive worldwide sugar prices and other economic pressures threatened Hawaiʻi's sugar industry from the beginning, and as the 20th Century progressed, the plantations began to merge, then shut down one by one. Finally, in the mid-1990s, sugar on the Hāmākua Coast was completely phased out. Today, residents along the coast are actively exploring new land uses, from timber to cattle, ginger root to exotic fruits.

Exploring the Hāmākua Coast
Hawaiʻi Island is nicknamed the Big Island for good reason. The Hāmākua Coast region alone is almost as large as the state of Rhode Island. A nonstop drive from end to end takes about an hour, but add time

at the many irresistible stops along the way and it easily becomes a full- or even multi-day experience. The area's emergence as a visitor destination explains the proliferation of excellent bed-and-breakfast lodgings up and down the coast.

The Hāmākua Coast and its main highway run approximately north-south, with 13,790-foot Mauna Kea to the west and the Pacific Ocean to the east. Although maps and highway signs refer primarily to "north" and "south," local residents give directions differently. As is only natural on an island, local directions refer to *mauka* (toward the mountains) and *makai* (toward the sea), as well as to major landmarks and end points—Honoka'a (northern) and Hilo (southern). Accordingly, directions in this book use the four directions as *mauka*, *makai*, Honoka'a and Hilo.

Highway signs and some maps often refer to the *ahupua'a* and historic districts. Highway 19 and an earlier coastal road interweave all along the coast. Although it is numbered or described on some maps as Hawai'i Belt Road or the New Māmalahoa Highway, local folks call Highway 19 simply "the main highway" or "the belt highway." Built beginning in the late 1940s after the demise of the Hawaii Consolidated Railway, Highway 19 covers over much of the rail route as well as parts of the older highway. This earlier road, dating back to the early 1900s, is called the Old Māmalahoa Highway or just "the old highway" and passes through many of the older communities and some of the coast's most scenic points of interest. Directions in this book refer to Highway 19 and Old Māmalahoa Highway.

Brown-and-white Hilo-Hāmākua Heritage Coast signs—with the sugar cane tassel logo—along Highway 19 indicate main visitor attractions and are marked in this book's gatefold map. The map also provides a locator resource for most of the photographs in the book. Also useful are the small highway signs positioned along the *makai* side of Highway 19, indicating mileage from Hilo Airport. These are also indicated in this book, as M5, for example, for Mile 5.

The boxed numbers in captions in these pages denote locations on the foldout map at the back cover. While many of these sites can be visited today, note that many others are private property and cannot be entered without permission.

Touring Tips

Other than at the Hāmākua Coast end-point towns of Hilo and Honoka'a, only one gas station—at Mile 25 and not always open—is to be found along Highway 19, located approximately halfway along the coast at Laupāhoehoe. Public restrooms are available at the Laupāhoehoe Train Museum (M25), across Highway 19 from that single gas station, and at businesses and parks on side roads.

Highway 19 is the only practical commuter route through the coast. Residents appreciate courteous and safe driving. A friendly thank-you toot may be the only time that a car horn is sounded. Care and consideration should be taken in parking, biking or walking along the highway, especially at narrow bridges. Large wide trucks and buses are common on Highway 19.

Frequent rains keep the coast's foliage green and its streams full, and motorists should be on the alert for wet or muddy pavement. Cliffs above roads and highways occasionally release loose rocks or even small landslides, especially during heavy rains.

Many side routes are privately owned and off limits to travelers. A KAPU sign means taboo—no trespassing. Caves and rock walls or platforms are often very sacred and private places for Native Hawaiian families and should be carefully respected. Disturbing them may be both illegal and dangerous.

Other hazards include animals and pedestrians. While the area's trails, cliffs, waterfalls, streams and beaches are tempting to explore, natural hazards can include flash floods, strong ocean currents, sudden large waves and even falling coconuts. Hāmākua

Coast waves can be large, powerful and unpredictable. Hikers, fishermen and others at the shoreline should never turn their backs on the ocean.

The Plantation Legacy
Most of *Exploring the Hāmākua Coast* is devoted to the sugar era—at least those years documented by photography—from the late 1800s to the transitional statehood era of the 1950s and '60s, when the isolated plantation camps morphed into self-contained communities. The photographs here reveal that, despite the remoteness and the relatively low income levels, plantation life was surprisingly diverse and sophisticated—full of much more than just the backbreaking day-to-day monotony of plantation work. The cultural sensitivities, friendships and optimism of that bygone era continue to enrich the Hāmākua Coast today. It is a very precious legacy indeed.

A Note About Usage
Diacritical marks affecting pronunciation—macrons and glottal stops used to clarify pronunciation—are used throughout this book (*i.e.*, Hawai'i, Pa'ahau). Such marks weren't commonly used in the plantation era, however, and all store, church, school and business names are included here in their original form (*i.e.*, Hawaii Consolidated Railway, Paahau Store).

6

9 **Nineteenth-Century Honoka'a**

In the 1880s, "downtown" Honoka'a was just a scattering of buildings. Today the area stretches from Pā'auhau in the south to the Āhualoa community in the *mauka* forest. This region has long been used for ranching and farming. In 1894, the ledgers of Honoka'a's Lawson Store reflected the cost of living—eggs for $.25 sold to the Honokaa Club, salmon for $.50 to W. Purdy, and fish for $.15 to Dr. Kamai. D. Forbs bought leggings for $6.00 and five pounds of coffee for $1.50.

Hawai'i State Archives

CHAPTER ONE
Honoka'a & Waipio Valley

Beginning and End

Both a gateway and a departure point, Honokaʻa is the biggest town on the Hāmākua Coast. Built along high bluffs overlooking the sea, it is steeped in the history and traditions of plantation life. With small-town charm and friendly people, Honokaʻa boasts one old-style hotel—the Hotel Honokaa Club—several bed-and-breakfast accommodations, homespun restaurants, shops, banks, churches, a health facility and an affordable golf course. The old Haina sugar mill, now inaccessible, is located *makai* on Lehua Street, down a steep road that also passes a coffee mill and artist colony where visitors are always welcome.

The approach to Honokaʻa town on Highway 19 from the Kamuela/Waimea direction offers several entry options. The main entry point is Plumeria Road, running *makai* (toward the sea) from the highway. Drivers arriving from the Hilo direction can turn at Māmane Street (Highway 240).

Honokaʻa offers visitor information, restaurants, gift shops, factory tours, and other attractions and services, as well as several sites of historic interest. At the Hilo end of town, for instance, Highway 240 passes the Honokaʻa High School campus on the *mauka* side and the Katsu Goto memorial on the *makai* side. An early Japanese immigrant to the Hāmākua Coast, Katsu Goto fought for better treatment for plantation workers and one morning was found hanged near this site.

Beautiful Waipiʻo Valley is located eight miles from downtown Honokaʻa at the end of Highway 240, where the Waipiʻo Valley Lookout presents one of the Big Island's most popular photo opportunities. Budget for a leisurely one-hour round trip to Waipiʻo and time to Honokaʻa.

10 * B. Ikeuchi & Sons

Opened in the 1920s, by Bunso Ikeuchi (above), B. Ikeuchi & Sons hardware store has been a landmark at Honokaʻa's
Waipiʻo end for generations. Photographed here ca. 1940, the store still operates today at the junction of Māmane
and Lehua Streets. A visit to Ikeuchi can be an experience in virtual time travel; it offers everything from parts
for an ancient kerosene stove to a new microwave somewhere in the stock stacked high between floor and ceiling.

Ikeuchi Family Collection

* See map, inside back cover.

▌▌ Honoka'a Flood

This photo was probably taken after a devastating flood in 1935 that covered downtown Honoka'a with mud during a rainstorm. Here some of the mud is scraped and cleared near the Waipi'o Valley end of downtown Māmane Street. Before Māmane Street was paved, an annual horse race was staged in this area. In the years around 1925, the winner was usually Mr. Hasegawa's famous champion, Candy Girl.

North Hawai'i Community Federal Credit Union

▇ Honokaa Theatre

On November 18, 1939, a crowd gathers at the Honokaa Theatre's grand opening. The facility was nicknamed the Doc Hill Theater after the prominent entrepreneur who owned a chain of Big Island movie houses. The building still stands today on the *makai* side of Māmane Street in downtown Honoka'a, with a shop at street level and balconied apartments above. It was completed at the same time as the Honokaa People's Theatre, called the Tanimoto Theater after its owner, which still shows movies today at is original location just to the north of this building.

North Hawai'i Community Federal Credit Union Collection

12 Old Honoka'a Town

Honoka'a today still boasts the rustic charm evidenced here ca. 1920. The AhFoo Restaurant operated in this impressive structure which still stands across from the North Hawai'i Community Federal Credit Union on Māmane Street. (The credit union building had earlier housed the Lawson Store.) The sidewalks with two-step curbs on the *mauka* side made it more accessible to passengers in horse-drawn wagons. *Hal Yamato Collection*

Yamato's General Store & Garage

Yamato's General Store & Garage hasn't changed much since this summer day in 1920. Today it is home to a variety of shops across Māmane Street from the Salvation Army, located in a former hotel. The Yamatos were also farmers and ran a Japanese language school up *mauka* in the village of Āhualoa. *Hal Yamato Collection*

14 Telephone Technology

Placing a phone call could be a complicated process in Honokaʻa in the 1930s. The caller picked up the home phone receiver—which had no dialing capability—and was automatically connected to this operator in town, wearing her horn-like mouthpiece and facing a panel of phone plugs. She then placed the call, plugged in the connection and could even listen in on the conversation. For a long-distance call she rang another operator, probably in Hilo, for connection to a long-distance line.

Paul Christensen Collection

8 Haina Sugar Mill

Plantation residences, as here at Haina in 1946, were often built close by the industrial activities of the sugar mill. Cane harvested from surrounding fields was washed, chopped, squeezed and processed, to the accompaniment of intrusive smells and sounds, day and night, from muddy diesel trucks and rumbling machines. This mill was converted into an electric power plant in the 1990s, using a powerful jet turbine engine. Honoka'a Landing was located on the shoreline near the mill. Many of the residents of Haina moved up to Honoka'a town in the late 20th Century.

Paul Christensen Collection

7 Honoka'a Landing

Honoka'a Landing at Haina, *makai* of Honoka'a town, was used mostly for liquid transfers, using a rubber pipe floating on the ocean surface between ship and shore. Oil came in and molasses went out. Molasses was a liquid version of sugar derived from the milling process. Facilities for loading raw sugar were located at nearby Pā'auhau and Kukuihaele Landings. Honoka'a literally means "rolling bay" [as in stones] and perhaps refers to the characteristics of this shoreline area. *R.J. Baker/Hawai'i State Archives*

6 Cane Field Firing Range

During World War II, local Filipino and Portuguese men served in a home guard called the Hawaii Rifles, protecting bridges and preparing against possible invasion by imperial Japanese forces. This guard was organized along the coast and made up mostly of volunteer aliens who could not serve in the U.S. military. Here they practice marksmanship in a cleared area of a cane field overlooking the ocean along the way to Waipi'o Valley. The Big Island was never invaded during the war. *Paul Christensen Collection*

5 Kukuihaele Landing

Cargo was moved between ships and Kukuihaele Landing with a system of cables. One end of a cable was attached to a buoy anchored in the ocean floor about 1,000 feet offshore; the other end to a building at the cliff top. Ships then anchored under this cable between the two ends. Cargo was suspended from the cable and another was used to pull it up or lower it down. Sugar was the primary cargo at this landing, shown here ca. 1930. Occasionally, plantation workers were invited to dine aboard ship. *Paul Christensen Collection*

4 **Kukuihaele Breakwater**

Shown here ca. 1915, this small breakwater and pier were used to load barges with boulders quarried from the Kukuihaele cliff. These boulders were used in constructing the large breakwater at Hilo Bay. A tsunami later destroyed this site. The quarry work, as well as construction of the long Hāmākua Ditch for Big Island irrigation needs, populated Kukuihaele village with workers in the early 1900s. The village boasted 14 stores, two bakeries, two barbers, two pool halls, Kukuihaele School, a Japanese language school, a saloon and the Pacific Sugar Mill. *Hawai'i State Archives*

3 Hāpai Kō at Kukuihaele

Workers harvest cane ca. 1930 photo in a Kukuihaele field near the Waipiʻo Valley Lookout ca. 1930.
At harvest, the dried cane leaves were often burned and the remaining juicy stalks cut down and trimmed
into segments. They were then bundled and tied with the long green leaves. The bundles of sugar (*kō*)
were carried (*hāpai*) to wooden flumes that were temporarily set up in the field, full of rushing water that
transported the harvest down to the mill. It was messy work among all the black ash. *Paul Christensen Collection*

▮ Waipiʻo Valley

The beachfront of Waipiʻo Valley, ca. 1880, is barren of the ironwood trees that line it today. It was common in the early 1900s for Kukuihaele children to walk up and down the long steep road to play in the pristine valley, sometimes making the trip down on a Sunday morning and returning after lunch. The beach was pebbly and the surf was rough, so it was more of a wading beach than a place for swimming or fishing. Tsunamis, storms and vegetation have changed this landscape considerably over the years. *Hawaiʻi State Archives*

▌ Waipi'o Valley 1880

Waipi'o Valley before the turn of the century was in a period of transition from ancient Hawai'i to the era of plantation immigrants and cultural diversity. The ancient valley was a gathering place for chiefs and the legendary site for the royal seat of authority, for the king of the island of Hawai'i. The late 1800s, however, saw the introduction of new crops such as Japanese lotus roots (*hasu*) and watercress that contrasted with the traditional taro plants. Several stores, a Chinese temple, churches and a public school were also built in the valley. *Hawai'i State Archives*

▎ Outrigger Canoes

Two streams ran through Waipi'o Valley in the early 1900s. Boats were used to cross over them, although certain areas were shallow enough to wade across. Japanese fishermen caught *dojo*, a small eel-like fish, to make into *miso* soup. The *'o'opu* fish was boiled, stewed in a soup of soy sauce and sugar, or broiled over charcoal with salt seasoning. Here ca. 1880, Hawaiian outrigger canoes traverse the valley's calm waters. *Hawai'i State Archives*

2 Hi'ilawe Falls

The awesome 1,000-foot Hi'ilawe Falls of Waipi'o Valley has long inspired travelers, artists and musicians. Here in 1880, a Western-style structure stands deep in the valley. Legend has it that the earth of the upper valley was red from the blood of the demigod Maui, after the god Kanaloa had thrown him upon the rocks. Other legends speak of a royal palace from which the island was ruled and of runners that traveled as messengers to the hundreds of chiefs in all the districts on the island.
Hawai'i State Archives

15 Paauhau Store

Pā'auhau was once a mill, a camp and a landing that stood south of Honoka'a on the *makai* side of Highway 19.
Here is the Pā'auhau plantation store ca. 1925, with a post office on the porch and an oil house to the left.
Today this building is a private residence, and Honoka'a town now dominates business activity in this district. *Mauka*
of Highway 19 is the upper section of old Pā'auhau, including Old Māmalahoa Highway and the former plantation
manager's mansion. Chiefs Kamehameha and Keoua fought a famous battle in this area. *Hawai'i State Archives*

16 Pa'auilo Plantation Store

This photo of the old plantation store, ca. 1950, shows buildings that still stand today near the pedestrian overpass *mauka* of the main highway. It is now the site of a grocery store. Here the U.S. Post Office appears on the Hilo side of the store and a former plantation meat processing facility on the Hāmākua side. The one-time plantation manager's mansion stood on the grassy hill on the Hāmākua side of this building. *Gomes Family Collection*

Chapter Two
Pa'auilo

The End of the Rail

Pa'auilo is a large rural community stretching from *mauka* to *makai* and bisected by Highway 19. This was the end of the line for the old Hawaii Consolidated Railway, the Hilo-based railroad that served the plantation communities in the early 20th Century. The line's northern terminus was built in lower Pa'auilo in 1913, and a shortage of funds precluded any further rail extension north to Honoka'a.

Coffee trees were grown extensively here in the early 1900s, until farming and production shifted to the other side of the Big Island and Kona coffee became the world-famous gourmet product that it is today. For most of the past century, Pa'auilo's economy was driven primarily by sugar and cattle.

Pa'auilo has always boasted a sort of an Old West ambience. It was a rowdy place during World War II, when U.S. Marines based in the town of Waimea (Kamuela) visited Pa'auilo for R&R. In those days payday always brought visits by enterprising Honolulu prostitutes.

Today the old neighborhoods *makai* of Highway 19 still retain much of the physical character of the early Hāmākua Coast plantation days. Outside of town, vast acres of eucalyptus tree farms cover the slopes, ready for harvest after seven years' growth. Here, too, the rare *'io*, Hawaiian hawk, can often be seen circling gently overhead.

The center of Pa'auilo is marked by the pedestrian overpass (M37) on Highway 19. Local-style snacks are available in the old Pa'auilo Plantation Store building next to the overpass. Next to the old store are the former meat-processing facilities and manager's mansion. Old downtown Pa'auilo is located *mauka* upslope in the northern Honoka'a direction on Highway 19.

North of Pa'auilo, on the *mauka* side of Highway 19 at Kalōpā (M40), is a winding road that climbs to Kalōpā State Park. Here are picnic facilities and overnight cabins nestled among tall trees.

South on Highway 19 in the Hilo direction is tiny Kuka'iau village (M35). Nearby 'O'ōkala Village (M30) is hidden *makai* of the highway. The village once had its own sugar mill until the plantation merged with others at this northern end of the Hāmākua Coast.

16 Old Paʻauilo Town

Left to right: Ryoichi Takamune, Hatashi Takamune and Arthur Nahm pose in Paʻauilo ca. 1929, beneath signs for a tailor, a chop sui restaurant and Standard Oil Products. Vacant now, a few of these buildings still stand today. Downtown Paʻauilo also offered a bar and a movie theater with wooden seats. The utility pole shows that modern technology had already come to this remote, rural community, while many automobiles already traversed the streets of Paʻauilo. *Nakahara Family Collection*

16 Paʻauilo School

While this 1940 graduation photo at Paʻauilo School shows only boys, it was also common for Hāmākua Coast girls of the day to complete their studies. Principal Huglan stands with the proud graduates. In earlier decades, students on the Hāmākua Coast were only expected to attend school through the eighth or ninth grade. Only the more ambitious ones went on to high school, often boarding there, while a few went on to college. In the 1950s, Paʻauilo graduates usually went to Honokaʻa High or to St. Joseph's, a Catholic school in Hilo. *Gomes Family Collection*

16 Pa'auilo Hongwanji

Buddhist residents of Pa'auilo hold a happy and festive *chigo* parade ceremony, ca. 1955, at Pa'auilo Hongwanji, apparently commemorating the completion of the temple building. On such occasions children dressed in beautiful kimonos and wore ceremonial makeup. Built from a large converted military quonset hut, the Buddhist temple still stands *mauka* of Pa'auilo town. It was bought and transported to this spot from a former U.S. Marine base in the town of Waimea (Kamuela). *Nakahara Family Collection*

Hore Hore Bushi

In the 1930s, when the sugar cane crop was nearly ready to harvest, the older dried leaves were stripped away by hand, leaving just the juicy stalks and the shorter green leaves on top. The paper-like older leaves had a protective coat of short needles that could prick the skin, while the leaf edges were serrated with similar barbs.

The Japanese plantation women, who usually handled the stripping chores, called this job *hore hore* (ho-reh ho-reh). This was apparently a Japanese pronunciation of the Hawaiian word *hole* (ho-leh) which means "to peel or strip."

The women protected themselves from the hot tropical sun with footwear, leggings, thick skirts, heavy aprons, long-sleeved shirts, thick kerchiefs and hats. They wore gloves called *te-oi*, or "hand covering," in Japanese.

For these Japanese immigrants, contracts to work *hore hore* in the cane fields were usually multi-year commitments. Out in the fields, the women had ample time to contemplate their decision to travel to mysterious Hawai'i from their homes in Japan. What emotions did they feel: regret, self-pity, home-sickness, frustration, desperation, hope, optimism?

Was working *hore hore* better than enduring the poor economic conditions in Japan at that time? One indication comes from the Hore Hore Bushi (song), a Japanese musical style sung a cappella in the plantation camps, in the same way the blues developed in the plantations of the southern U.S.

Former Pa'auilo resident Shigeko Miyashiro recalls her mother, Tsuru Hamasu, singing these verses of Hore Hore Bushi in 1935 at Pa'auilo Mauka camp:

Yukoka America? Kaeroka Nihon? Koko ga shian no, Hawai'i koku?
(Go to America? Return to Japan? What do I truly feel in Hawai'i?)

Nanno inga de Hawai'i ni kitaro hana no sakarimo kibi no naka.
(Why did I come to Hawai'i as a budding young flower to work in the cane field?)

Sanjugo sen no hore hore shoyo rya pakesan to moi moi suriyo akahi kala $1.
(Thirty-five cents to *hore hore*, or sleep with the Chinese man for one dollar?)

17 Cattle Branding

The Ramos family brands cattle in Paʻauilo Mauka in the early 1940s. Cattle ranching has been a big part of Paʻauilo life throughout the 20th Century, with ranches operating mostly in the *mauka* areas of the region. It wasn't uncommon for even young children to learn traditional cowboy skills such as roping and riding. Hāmākua Coast sugar plantations also needed skilled riders to work mules and tend beef cattle, and beef for local consumption was processed at the plantations' slaughterhouses. *Gomes Family Collection*

16 Homemade Fun

In a scene right out of small-town America, ca.1960, Pa'auilo natives Scott and Doreen Nakahara enjoy a ride in a wagon built by their father, real estate broker Thomas Nakahara. Today Scott is a dentist in Honoka'a and his sister is an educator on the mainland. Homemade toys were often more fun, and always more affordable, for Hāmākua Coast children. Primo Beer, brewed in Honolulu, was a local brand discontinued in the 1970s.

Nakahara Family Collection

34

16 Poison Car

This specialized railroad car, shown here at Pa'auilo in 1943, helped control weeds growing along the tracks.
The large storage tank in the center car held water mixed with chemical herbicides. The "poison car," as it was called,
was a Hawaii Consolidated Railway fixture along the Hāmākua Coast. *John O. May Collection / Laupāhoehoe Train Museum*

19 Laupāhoehoe Gulch

This appears to be Laupāhoehoe Gulch, ca. 1920, from a vantage point where Highway 19 now curves over Laupāhoehoe Stream. The Old Māmalahoa Highway meanders below and connects to Laupāhoehoe Point at the mouth of the stream. The plantings here were possibly hala trees or even coffee, which was once heavily cultivated on private farms in this area. The slope on the left is described by some long-timers as "Big Hill." In the 19th Century visitors traversed these difficult Hāmākua Coast gulches by foot or on horseback. *Pacific Tsunami Museum*

CHAPTER THREE
Laupāhoehoe & Pāpaʻaloa

Traveling Then and Now

Rail routes, small winding roads and treacherous trails were the ways to travel before Highway 19 was built; especially through tricky terrain like the three horseshoe-shaped gulches near the town of Laupāhoehoe: Kaʻawaliʻi Gulch (M29), Laupāhoehoe Gulch (M27) and Maulua Gulch (M22). At Mile 26 is an excellent overlook of Laupāhoehoe Point. *Lau* means "leaf" and *pāhoehoe* means "smooth lava flat," and the peninsula below does indeed suggest a flat, spreading "leaf" of lava. From this spot, one can picture the canoes, rowboats and sailing ships that challenged the point's pounding surf more than a century ago.

Nearby, on the *mauka* side of Highway 19, is the Laupāhoehoe Train Museum, site of the town's old train depot. The long concrete boarding platform is still visible at the side of the road, and the station master's home still stands as well, now chock-full of rail-era memorabilia.

The museum offers one of the few public restrooms on the mid-coast stretch of Highway 19, while the service station diagonally across Highway 19 from the museum offers the only gas between the two ends of the Hāmākua Coast.

The *mauka* turnoff south of the museum leads for approximately a half-mile on the Old Māmalahoa Highway, past the police/fire station, the post office, the old-time favorite Sakado Store, a stream bridge, the old Laupāhoehoe Dispensary, a Catholic church, homes and businesses, and Laupāhoehoe School. The old road then reconnects with Highway 19.

The town of Pāpaʻaloa is located to the south along Highway 19. Pāpaʻaloa's mill was operated by Laupāhoehoe Sugar Company, which ran from 1870 until it merged with Hamakua Sugar of Honokaʻa 100 years later. This mill stood near the edge of the seacliff, in the overgrown area below today's Papaaloa Store, located on the old road *makai* of Highway 19. This mom-and-pop retailer with the oiled wood floor sells literally everything from soup to nuts and many items in between, including local take-out foods and catered meals. Pāpaʻaloa's post office shares the building. The old road heads south past Papaaloa Hongwanji, the former plantation garage, and the ballpark and gym, before merging again with Highway 19 at Mile 24.

18 Laupāhoehoe Point

In the late 19th Century, when stone walls and thatched grass buildings were typical throughout the Hawaiian archipelago, Laupāhoehoe Point still appeared much as it did before Western contact. Taro and sweet potatoes were still widely grown in this area where Kamehameha the Great lived for a while as a young man. The waters here are treacherous, giving credence to the advanced skill that Native Hawaiians needed to navigate their canoes.

Pacific Tsunami Museum

18 **Laupāhoehoe Point, 1920**

A Protestant church, a Mormon church and a Jodo Buddhist temple served the community of Laupāhoehoe in the 1920s. The temple building is now in private use. The various congregations eventually relocated to higher ground. Animals were still heavily used in this early modern period, and a stable operated on the Point. A horse could carry a rider all the way to Hilo or Kamuela at about four miles per hour. *Hawai'i State Archives*

18 Old Laupahoehoe Post Office

The town's post office, ca. 1920, was located at Laupāhoehoe Point and housed some 50 post office boxes. Nonagenarian "Willie" Choy Hee remembers a courthouse, soda works, a general store, a coffee mill, a blacksmith shop and five small hotels on the Point. A Territorial government building was used for tax collection, while the boat landing nearby is still in use today. By the mid-1900s the post office had relocated to a new home near today's train museum and by the end of the century was replaced by the current post office. *Hawai'i State Archives*

18 Old Laupahoehoe School

The former Laupahoehoe School stands at right center before the devastating tsunami of 1946. The powerful waves surged as far inland as the long U-shaped building. Only the large gym *mauka* of the building still stands today. The concrete foundations of school buildings remain just *makai* of the large banyan tree that continues to grow. Pictured in the upper left corner is the school that was later relocated to higher ground. An early sugar mill once operated in the 1870s in the area at left, near where the peninsula meets the seacliff. *Pacific Tsunami Museum*

The Tsunami of 1946

On the Hāmākua Coast, April Fool's Day will always be remembered as the day in 1946 when a massive tsunami flooded over Laupāhoehoe Point. The ocean was behaving strangely that Monday morning. The sea level rose higher than normal, then receded farther than usual. Sea creatures flopped about on the drained ocean bottom near shore. Some of the school kids walked out to investigate.

Then the series of huge waves flooded in to shore, pushing people and buildings inland in frightening confusion. Many people were washed back out to sea; some were caught on bushes and trees. Others could only watch helplessly from further *mauka* in the valley and from the top of the cliff above Laupāhoehoe Point. The waves were less like typical surfing rollers and more like massive vertical walls of rumbling water, nearly as high as the shoreline trees and the lighthouse.

A few victims were able to float with the debris until they were rescued, while others were lost to the sea. Teachers' cottages located near shore, where a pavilion stands today, quickly floated off their foundations and were destroyed. Some of the teachers could not swim, and rescuers were unable to save everyone. Familiar faces were seen bobbing in the chaotic sea. Because all the boats in the area had also been destroyed, the two children and one teacher who had survived the tsunami drifted offshore until late afternoon, when they were finally rescued. (The following year, that teacher married the doctor who arrived in the rescue boat.)

When it was over, 16 students, four teachers and four other Laupāhoehoe residents were dead. The day of horror was marked by a memorial which now stands at Laupāhoehoe Point, and each year, services are held for those who were lost that day. The marker's inscription—In Memory of Those Who Lost Their Lives in the Tidal Wave, April 1, 1946—is followed by the names and ages of the tsunami's 24 victims.

20 Laupāhoehoe Train Station

The large Laupāhoehoe Train Station, photographed here ca. 1930, was razed after the 1946 demise of the Hawaii Consolidated Railway. Today only the concrete platform remains along the *mauka* side of Highway 19. The station master's impressive home stood just behind the station building and now serves as the Laupāhoehoe Train Museum, where rail cars, a small engine and assorted memorabilia are preserved and displayed. *Hilo Coast United Church of Christ*

46

20 **Holy Ghost Parade**
Catholics in Hāmākua Coast communities held Holy Ghost Parades to honor the Virgin Mary.
This Laupāhoehoe parade, ca. 1930, appears to be crossing a spot across Highway 19 from today's Train
Museum. A service station is now located to the right of the house and *makai* of the tracks. Laupāhoehoe's
event, usually held in summer, followed a route starting at the train station, then moving toward the center
of town in the Hilo direction along the Old Māmalahoa Highway. *Larry Ignacio Collection / Laupāhoehoe Train Museum*

20 A Filipino Funeral

A funeral in Laupāhoehoe illustrates the social situation of many young male plantation workers from the Philippines. Since few women emigrated, many of these men were bachelors, usually living in barracks at different camps along the Hāmākua Coast. Many of the early Filipino immigrants married Native Hawaiian women. Though workers' pay was relatively low, they were able to afford suits and shoes. The cross by the coffin reveals that this is the funeral of Antonio T. Caoagas, who died on January 8, 1934. *Laupāhoehoe Train Museum*

21 Peddler Truck

Peddlers like this one, ca. 1920, were common all along the Hāmākua Coast. Serving as convenient mobile stores, they offered residents a wide variety of goods—vegetables, candies, pastries and much more. Terada's store sold a popular long john doughnut with a creamy filling from its truck. Hasegawa's from Honoka'a carried candies, fabrics and sewing supplies. In later years, some areas enjoyed home deliveries of dry cleaning, fresh fish, shave ice (snow cones), ice cream and mail. Some residents on the coast could phone in grocery orders to their local stores for delivery.

Laupāhoehoe Train Museum

21 Bridge at Pāpaʻaloa

Dwarfed by massive timbers, railway workers erect a bridge in 1912 at Pāpaʻaloa, just *mauka* of town. This bridge has now been replaced with the Highway 19 bridge, covering over the old railway route. This area was surrounded by many smaller camps: Kaʻaiakea, Kapehu, Kīlau, Kihalani, Korean, Chinese, Spanish, Japanese, Hokama Camps and others. Some Russian immigrants, who liked to hunt, also lived up near the tree line of Mauna Kea.

Lucy Nuesca Collection/Laupāhoehoe Train Museum

50

22 Hakalau Plantation

Hakalau Plantation's mill, shown here (far right) in 1935, was built right at the treacherous shoreline of Hakalau Bay, with support facilities located above it in the village proper. The bay was a busy shipping port in the days of Hawaiʻi's inter-island sailing ships. Cattle, passengers and plantation freight went in and out for about five cents per item, big or small. The Hawaii Consolidated Railway line was later built just *mauka* of the mill area. In 1906, a section of track extended back from Hakalau Station to the mill, where two concrete warehouses still stand. *Hawaiʻi State Archives*

CHAPTER FOUR
Hakalau & Wailea

The Twin Towns

Hakalau Mill stood at the water's edge on the south side of the bay, below the bustling town with its train station, gym, photo studio, theaters, store, hospital and homes. Situated on Old Māmalahoa Highway off Highway 19, some of old Hakalau town remains today, including the post office operating in the lobby of the now-defunct theater. The impressive former plantation manager's home 24 stands *mauka* of the roadway; the grounds here once included a tennis court. Two concrete warehouses are also still standing on the *makai* side of the road, where an earlier post office served the little plantation community. This old Hakalau town can be found by turning *makai* off Highway 19 at the pedestrian overpass just south of the Hakalau Stream bridge.

From this same intersection, Old Māmalahoa Highway also runs *mauka* past homes, Hakalau Gym, the former school, a ballfield and tiny Wailea village. In Wailea, a one-time auto garage has become an art gallery, gift shop and bed-and-breakfast. A former bakery is now an incubator kitchen where local folks reproduce and sell delicacies from family recipes. In an earlier time, other stores, another service station, a bar, churches and a Japanese language school made Wailea a lively place.

From Wailea, the old road meanders down to sea level and Kolekole Park at the mouth of Kolekole Stream. This park is for picnicking, not swimming, since the rough water here can be hazardous.

Old Māmalahoa Highway merges with Highway 19 again at the Hilo end of the Kolekole Bridge. The Honoka'a end of the bridge once was the site of Wailea's own sugar mill, which opened in 1919 and operated until the 1940s, when its ownership merged with the Hakalau Plantation and it was subsequently razed.

29 **The Tsunami of '46**

This famous photo was taken by Shigcharu Furusho, who ran a photo studio behind the old Hakalau Gym nearby. Furusho also worked at the mill and was on duty when the big waves hit on April 1, 1946. He ran from the mill to his studio to get his camera and returned to chronicle the damage done. The framework in the background is the rail bridge that was widened into the current Highway 19 bridge. The normal shoreline appears at right. The water flow at top is the result of a broken flume. *Sugino Family Collection*

29 Hakalau Mill Rebuilds

The mill stands rebuilt after the 1946 tsunami. From time to time, the structure was also battered by storm waves, and employees had to exercise caution when working outside near the shoreline. Water-filled flumes (left and right) fed harvested cane into the mill from the seacliff. A chute from directly above was also in service for a short time. The mill's smokestack rose high above the cliff's edge. Deteriorated from years of use and the incessant salt spray, the facility was finally closed in the 1960s, when milling operations shifted to Pepeʻekeo. *Paul Christensen Collection*

23 Pounding Mochi

Mochitsuki or *mochi* pounding continues today as a traditional Japanese New Year's activity. Here bare-chested Rev. Bino Mamiya of Hakalau Jodo Mission takes his turn at pounding downstairs in the Buddhist Temple. The temple still stands today across from Hakalau Theater. Hoichi George Ueda is turning the *mochi* (rice paste), while Margie Furusho and Aiko Kikuchi also pound. This happy scene probably took place just before World War II, when Rev. Mamiya was forced into an internment camp with other Hāmākua Coast Japanese community leaders. *Sugino Family Collection*

27 Old Hakalau Post Office
The old Hakalau Post Office, shown here ca. 1940, stood near the top of the seacliff above the mill, sharing space
with the plantation store. The sign points *makai* toward Hakalau Hospital. Lumber from structures in this area
was later used to build the Hakalau Gym near the Hakalau Theater. From this point, the Old Māmalahoa Highway
continues down into the gulch, though that area is now restricted private property. *Sugino Family Collection*

25 Hakalau Theater

Today's Hakalau Post Office operates in the lobby of the former Hakalau Theater, built in 1931. At one time a hairdresser also ran a salon on the structure's second floor. Because the theater floor sloped in a bleachers-like configuration, local kids could sneak under the building and peek at movies from beneath the seats. A small bridge near the theater allowed trains to pass beneath it then branch off *makai* of the building on their journey to the mill.

Sugino Family Collection

Sugar Strikes

The sugar strike of 1946 hit hard—79 days of picketing and trying to make ends meet without paychecks. Every morning, you'd report to the union hall or to another assigned station. Besides walking the picket lines, making it as difficult as possible for the plantation's scabs to report to work, we were also expected to perform a few hours of community service each day—cutting trees for firewood, doing odd jobs, whatever needed to be done. Fortunately for my family, we had money saved and a thriving vegetable garden, so were able to weather the strike with a minimum of hardship.

When the boycott ended, appropriately just before Thanksgiving, the workers found that their wages had generally doubled. Ten different grades of employees were established, from unskilled beginner to skilled veteran. Gone were most of the plantation perquisites—the free housing, water, electricity and medical care. But now we could better afford these basics on our own, without such dependence on the plantation bosses.

The next big strike was called in the spring of 1958, when the lowest grade field workers were still making only $1.12 an hour and fringe benefits were minimal. This one lasted a whopping 128 days, but we were much better prepared than in '46. We organized a soup kitchen at the community center and set up committees to cook or chop firewood or help in other ways. Food was prepared and delivered to families living in outlying areas. Credit unions extended loans to strikers.

I served the cause as an appraiser. I made the rounds to find work for strikers, who would then be sent off to clear a pasture, build a storage shed, paint a building, fix a car engine or plant cane for an independent grower. The client would then pay the union, if not in money then with a cow or a pig.

But in the end, all the *pilikia* (trouble) was worth it. By the '90s, Hawai'i's sugar workers were being paid almost $8 an hour in the two lowest grades and more than $10 an hour in the two highest. While that may seem low compared to tradesmen or other skilled workers, it was considered very high indeed by agricultural standards.

—The late Yasushi "Scotch" Kurisu, mill worker and International Longshoremen's and Warehousemen's Union official, in his memoir, Sugar Town

25 **26** **The Big Strike of '46**
Picket lines snaked in front of the old Hakalau Gym and Hakalau Theater, when members of the
International Longshoremen's and Warehousemen's Union boycotted the plantation for 79 days in 1946.
Razed by the 1970s, the gym was built ca. 1927 with lumber taken in the dismantling of the former plantation
store (page 56). Shigeharu Furusho's photo studio was located in the back of this old gym, which also
housed the Tatsuhara Barber Shop and, later on, the Morimoto Barber Shop. *Minoru Kodama Collection*

31 **Hakalau Train Station**
Hakalau Station was located *makai* of the theater. In 1935 the station boasted a well-balanced turntable,
allowing a few strong men to turn a rail car around. Here the main coastline track curved *makai* and merged with
the side track to Hakalau Mill. Mrs. John M. Ross, wife of a Scottish plantation manager in the early 1900s, is credited
with planting the countless palms and colorful trees that still grow throughout this area. *Minoru Kodama Collection*

30 Hakalau Hospital

This 26-bed hospital building was considered large for a plantation community. It stood close to the cliff *makai* of the mill's concrete warehouse. The late Yasushi "Scotch" Kurisu remembered the hospital being staffed by one physician, nurses, cooks, a pharmacist and a laundryman. This facility was highly regarded, especially in comparison to smaller clinics sometimes staffed by medical amateurs who would, for example, give the same treatment for different ailments. Shown here in 1920, Hakalau Hospital stands near a plantation-run library (right). *Sugino Family Collection*

28 The Rat Man

Mr. Kikuchi was a "rat man" for the Hakalau Plantation. His job was to catch the rodents and deliver them to government health officials who checked them for diseases such as bubonic plague. Rats were also a major problem for sugar plantations because they often chewed into ripe cane. The Hāmākua Coast variety could grow quite large, and dead rats were sometimes found floating in drinking water tanks next to plantation camp homes.

Sugino Family Collection

32 Kolekole Bridge

The intricate center supports of this railway bridge at Kolekole were destroyed by the 1946 tsunami. The bridge was later converted to support automobile traffic, with two surviving spans of Hilo's Wailuku River Railroad Bridge used in the rebuilding effort. Those spans can best be seen today from ground level. The Wailea Mill stood near the Honoka'a end of the bridge, *mauka* of Highway 19.

Pacific Tsunami Museum

Sugar Flumes: Fun but Dangerous

The practice of using flumes to transport harvested sugar cane stalks was borrowed from Pacific Northwest lumber operations of the early 20th Century. Hāmākua Coast plantations used wood and aluminum formed into large gutters, either U-shaped or V-shaped. Area streams were partially diverted into these flumes to provide constant water flow, which made them mossy and very slippery and also prevented the wood from drying out.

The field workers harvested cane by hand-cutting stalks with cane knives into segments several feet long, then bundling them with the long cane leaves and tossing them into the flumes for delivery further downslope. If no one was watching at the end of a shift, a ride in the flume provided a quicker commute home. Plantation kids were also tempted to ride in the fast-moving water, either atop the bundles of sliding cane or sitting right in the flumes—which often resulted in splinters in uncomfortable places.

But the greater danger of riding flumes was that of being swept out of control down to the mill, where heavy machinery was washing, chopping and grinding the stalks. Watchmen were stationed along some flumes to watch for cane snags, and some plantations built little shacks equipped with crank telephones, used to call the mill in the event of such problems.

Retired worker "Belly" Yugawa of Honomū recalls an incident in the 1960s when a young girl fell into a flume that fed the Hakalau Mill. The girl's mother frantically phoned the mill, and Belly ran out to the flume at a point just in front of the processing machinery. Another worker had just missed grabbing the girl further upslope. Belly jumped into the flume and caught her in time, a moment of great relief for both the girl and the workers.

32 Wailea Mill

Shuttered and dilapidated here in 1947, three years after it ceased operations and just before it was dismantled, the Wailea Mill in its heyday produced as much as 5,700 tons of raw sugar a year. The Wailea Milling Company was founded in 1919 by a businessman from Hiroshima, Japan, to process cane grown mostly by small independent growers. By the 1940s, most of the area's cane was being processed by C. Brewer & Company's big Hakalau Mill, a mile up the coast, and in 1944 the smaller operation merged with the larger. Some of the Wailea Mill's equipment was then transferred to Hakalau, while some was sold to sugar plantations in the Philippines. *Yasushi Kurisu Collection*

65

33 Honomū Landing

Shown here ca. 1920, this dangerous coastal landing was used by Honomu Sugar Company. It was built at a site *makai* and downslope from today's Honomū town turnoff from Highway 19. An incline cable rail system with a small steam engine called a "donkey" shuttled freight between upslope and the landing, which handled approximately 11,000 tons of plantation freight annually, including 6,700 tons of raw sugar bound for Hilo. Most non-plantation freight was transported overland to and from Hilo. *Ishii Family Collection*

CHAPTER FIVE

Honomū

Soldiers and Sugar

With its many charming shops and eateries, Honomū today stands in stark contrast to the rowdy outpost of World War II, when U.S. Army soldiers camped just *mauka* of town and the lineup of retail establishments included three liquor stores. Before the war, Honomū was a bustling plantation village with a shoemaker, barber, tailor, bakeries, noodle shop, gas station, churches, schools and markets.

Today, friendly Honomū offers gifts, memorabilia, gourmet meals, local favorite foods, fine art and a community computer center where travelers can check their e-mail. But Honomū may be best known to visitors as the gateway to ʻAkaka Falls, the popular attraction at the end of Highway 220. The 66-acre ʻAkaka Falls State Park includes a paved footpath that meanders through lush tropical greenery and offers views of both 450-foot ʻAkaka Falls and 400-foot Kahuna Falls.

Honomū and ʻAkaka Falls can be accessed from Highway 19 by taking the turnoff in the *mauka* direction to Highway 220 (M13), where it passes through a deep cut flanked by steep embakments. This was a former rail cut; the former Honomu Sugar Company railroad warehouse still stands on the *makai* side of Highway 19, near the turnoff. A Hawaii Consolidated Railway passenger station once stood on the Hilo side of the warehouse at the curve in the road. Highway 220 climbs steeply from this turnoff and levels where it connects to the Old Māmalahoa Highway. The large store at this intersection is the former Honomū Sugar Company Plantation store (page 70).

34 Honomū Mill

Shown here ca. 1920, the mill was located just *makai* of the Honomū turnoff from Highway 19. It was so hot inside Honomū Mill that in the 1930s one worker—a man named Kubota who shoveled *bagasse* (dried crushed cane stalks) into the sugar boilers—usually worked naked. His co-workers regularly had to yell to Kubota to dress whenever visitors came to call. During World War II, U.S. Army machine gunners were stationed at the cliff near the mill, and the sound of test firing could often be heard in the town of Honomū. The mill was closed in 1948 and later dismantled.

Ishii Family Collection

35 **Honomu Plantation Store**

The Honomū Plantation Store, shown here ca. 1920, was later called the Kayumangui Store. It still stands today where the turnoff road meets Old Māmalahoa Highway. In the late 1940s the store offered a range of goods from everyday necessities to a fabulous new luxury—an electric refrigerator! Along the stream near this store were once a small hydroelectric generator and a quarry. Kids had a favorite swimming hole near here called Kūkae (excreta) Pond for the questionable matter from a nearby sewage outfall floating on its surface. *Ishii Family Collection*

36 **Honomū Stone Quarry**

The quarry was located along the Old Māmalahoa Highway in a valley *mauka* of the Plantation Store. The facility was the primary source for the gravel used in paving the town's commercial area and for repairing roads. The "powder men"—those who handled the explosives in such quarries—had one of the most dangerous jobs on any sugar plantation. The small railway was used to transport equipment at the Honomū Quarry in the 1920s. A high flume stands in the background. *Ishii Family Collection*

Life in Honomū

In the early 1900s, a Native Hawaiian of royal lineage sold land in what is now downtown Honomū to Hideo Ishigo's father, Inokichi, for $5,000. Before immigrating to Hawai'i, Inokichi Ishigo had acquired business experience working at a *sake* (rice wine) factory in Fukuoka, Japan. In Honomū, Inokichi opened Ishigo Bakery on his parcel of land and taught himself the bakery business, baking bread and producing Japanese pastries such as *manju, senbei* and *umpan*. He bought a damaged Model T, stripped off the back and converted it into a flatbed truck for peddling his pastries in the plantation communities. Later Hideo joined the family business. The landmark bakery site and adjoining buildings still stand in downtown Honomū, occupied now by newer businesses.

Today, Hideo Ishigo explains that such home delivery was very popular along the Hāmākua Coast. One Honomū dairy delivered milk in glass bottles, chocolate milk included, as late as the 1950s.

Ishigo also recalls the role of matchmakers in the 1930s. As they did back in Japan, such people offered their services as go-betweens for shy young Japanese men and women. Some did it for personal satisfaction, while others charged for the service. Matchmaking required many subtle considerations. Japanese families in the early 1900s were both picky and very conservative. What's more, these families had emigrated from various prefectures in Japan, and it was much preferred that young people date those from their home areas. A couple from different prefectures, in fact, was considered *hapa*—Hawaiian for "half," or mixed blood—and such relationships were considered quite controversial. Eyebrows were raised even higher by more distinct "mixing"— between those from the far southern prefecture of Okinawa and other areas, for example, or, even more dramatic, between Japanese and non-Japanese couples. Such pressures slowly eased by the time third-generation Japanese began to date and inter-marry with other ethnic groups in the 1960s and '70s.

What did couples consider a big night on the town earlier in the 20th Century? According to Hideo Ishigo, it was a movie date up the coast at the Hakalau Theater.

37 Paving Downtown Honomū

A Hawai'i County dump truck unloads gravel in downtown Honomū ca. 1920. The barrels probably contain the tar used to pave Old Māmalahoa Highway. Most of the storefronts at rear are still standing today, as is the Tanimoto Theater, built in 1931. In its early days the Tanimoto screened silent movies, with local talent adding dramatic commentary. Honomū's Tanimoto family also operated theaters elsewhere on the Big Island. At one time, a plantation flume crossed directly over this section of Honomū's main street. *Ishii Family Collection*

38 Akita Store

Akita Store was a Honomū landmark in the early 1940s. The operation encompassed a grocery store, bar, gas station and soda fountain, where a banana split cost about 30 cents. This was a popular stop for both local people and for the U.S. Army soldiers stationed at Honomū during World War II. Daily sampan bus (page 118) service was provided for transport of older students to Hakalau School for $2 to $3 a month. There were many such combination gas stations and stores along Old Māmalahoa Highway. This building was later destroyed by fire. *Yugawa Family Collection*

39 Honomū Hongwanji
Honomū Hongwanji has been a Shin Buddhist temple serving Japanese immigrants in Honomū for more than a century. This temple, photographed ca. 1940, was built in 1922 to replace an earlier one. At one time it also housed a Japanese language school and a judo hall. Today it continues to serve the area's Buddhist community along with Honomū Henjoji (Odaisan), a Shingon Buddhist temple located nearby. Summers are especially lively in Honomū with festive *bon* dances. *Yugawa Family Collection*

39 Sumo Tournament

Japanese sumo wrestling was popular in Hāmākua Coast plantation communities such as Onomea and Honomū. Here in 1920, the Honomū team displays its impressive attire at a sumo ring, probably located on the grounds of Honomū Hongwanji. The better wrestlers imported their ceremonial aprons from Japan. A Native Hawaiian man of the time wrestled under the name of Dairiki. First-generation (*issei*) Japanese immigrants brought with them many traditional physical arts such as sumo, *kendo* (fencing), judo and karate. *Ishii Family Collection*

39 Shibai

A form of Japanese melodrama, *shibai* was also a big draw in the Hāmākua Coast's Japanese communities. The elaborate costumes, makeup, props and performances by local residents contrasted sharply with the day-to-day rigors of plantation life. Here, ca. 1930, Tetsuo Yugawa (right) plays an archer in long-ago Japan, possibly on the Honomū Hongwanji stage. Twice a year or so, an old bus traveled through the neighborhoods, as those inside the bus pounded on drums, yelled "Shibai!" and passed out leaflets to advertise upcoming performances. *Yugawa Family Collection*

40 Honomū Japanese Christian Church

The Hilo Coast United Church of Christ, formerly the Honomū Japanese Christian Church, was first located near today's Honomū Gym ball field. It was founded in 1894 by its revered pastor, Shiro Sokabe, who launched a number of beneficial community projects such as the Honomū Gijuku, a home and boarding school for children. The church, shown here ca. 1930, eventually consolidated congregations from Pāpa'ikou, Pepe'ekeo and Hakalau. A beautiful modern chapel was built in 1993 on the present site, *makai* of the gym on Old Māmalahoa Highway. *Ishii Family Collection*

30 **Cultural Exchange**
Old meets new in Honomū. Driver's licenses weren't required on the Big Island in the 1920s. A would-be car owner could simply visit a Hilo dealership, pay in full and drive off in a new Packard or Model T. The winding drive from Honomū to Hilo on Old Māmalahoa Highway took a little less than two hours. The lady wears traditional Japanese formal attire, probably a silk kimono and white *tabi* footwear. *Yugawa Family Collection*

Howitzer Company 299th Infantry - Honomu, Hawaii. Hilo Photo Works June 27 1929

41 Honomū's National Guard

In 1929 Honomū's population of several thousand was enough to support the Howitzer Company 299th Infantry National Guard. Here, flanked by a small cannon and a water-cooled machine gun, Sgt. Alex Akita sits with the unit's plaque in the front row. At the beginning of World War II, Japanese men were kicked out of the National Guard but were later able to join specialized units such as the much-decorated Japanese-American 442nd Regimental Combat Team. The 299th armory was located *mauka* of the yard behind Honomū Gym. *Yugawa Family Collection*

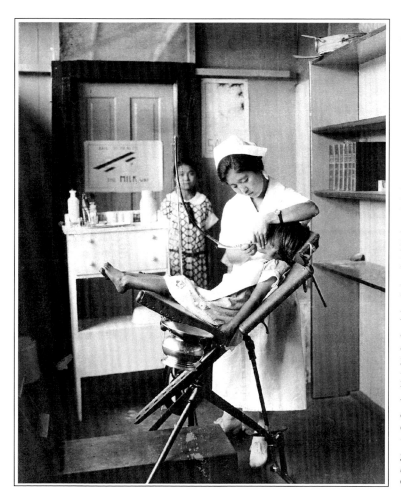

Dental Hygiene

Traveling dental hygienist E.Y. Ito made frequent visits to Honomu School in 1925. She used a portable folding examination chair set up in front of the principal's door. Her tools included a small rubber suction cup dusted with powder to clean students' teeth. A poster reminds students to "Drink Milk" for strong teeth. During Americanization efforts, "Speak American" posters were used to influence immigrant children. Honomu School was comprised of grades one through eight and was located *mauka* of today's Honomū Gym. The Class of '22 graduated four girls and ten boys.

Hilo Coast United Church of Christ

41 **Baseball in Honomū**

In the 1920s, baseball leagues in the Territory of Hawai'i were often organized by ethnicity. Honomū had Portuguese and Filipino teams, a Puerto Rican club called the Corsairs and two Japanese teams—the Aces and the Asahi. The Honomū Japanese Baseball Club shown here in 1925 was part of a plantation league for young adults, hosting games on the field next to the Honomu Gym that is still in use today. Among those who played for manager Kentaro Ishii (coat and tie) were his sons, Tom and Yutaka (front, center and right). *Ishii Family Collection*

Plowing Tractor

Kentaro Ishii, a Honomu Sugar Company mechanic, stands at center, ca. 1920, next to a tractor and disc plow used to break up the hardened surfaces of recently harvested cane fields. The worker seated at the rear manned a control to raise or lower the plowing implement as needed. Gasoline-powered equipment represented a vast improvement over the animal-powered variety previously used by Hāmākua Coast plantations. *Ishii Family Collection*

42 Fishing for Bonog

In the 1950s, the goby was a common catch in streams along the Hāmākua Coast. The fish went by other names, too, reflecting the cultural diversity of the plantation camps. It was ʻoʻopu in Hawaiian and bonog in the Ilocano Filipino dialect. Some called it gori, a Japanese pronunciation of "goby," while others called it kabosh. Anastacio Castro, Corby Sibayan and Felix Agamata are some of the proud fishermen displaying big ones caught near the town of Pepeʻekeo. The goby is now an endangered species. *Cabatu Family Collection*

CHAPTER SIX

Pepe'ekeo & Onomea

The Remnants of Sugar

The town of Pepeʻekeo (M11) appears suddenly to travelers driving south on Highway 19, at a point where the city of Hilo can be seen in the distance and, beyond that, sometimes even the far-off smoke from Kīlauea volcano (or a red glow after dark). Near the ocean here is the old Pepeʻekeo sugar mill, now converted into a coal-driven power plant that helps serve the Big Island's electrical needs.

Also at Pepeʻekeo is the *makai* turnoff to the four-mile Scenic Route along Old Māmalahoa Highway. A popular visitor lure, the Scenic Route passes through some of the most memorable shoreline scenery in the Hawaiian Islands, especially in the Onomea Bay area. The 40-acre valley behind this beautiful bay is now the site of the Hawaiʻi Tropical Botanical Garden, which has welcomed visitors to view its streams, waterfalls and more than 2,000 species of tropical plants since 1984.

Above Onomea Bay, the large area *makai* of Highway 19 at Mile 9 was once bustling Onomea Camp. This plantation town included neighborhoods informally called Japanese Camp, Filipino Camp and Puerto Rican Camp, as well as the mill, stable, train station, ballpark with grandstand, community clubhouse, Shinto shrine, a house used as a multi-denominational Buddhist chapel, clinics, stores, a Japanese language school with teacher's cottage, basketball gym, blacksmith, lumberyard, boarding houses, community bathhouses and graveyards.

An early 20th-Century plantation laborer's home was usually made of rough-sawn lumber and a corrugated iron roof, its interior walls covered with newspaper and white paper. One neighborhood in the Onomea area boasted a neat row of outhouses and laundry rooms all serviced by a regularly flushing sewer line.

Highway 19 crosses the long Hanawi Stream bridge just south of Onomea on the approach to Pāpaʻikou. In the gulch below, the view from here in the early 20th Century would have included women washing laundry in the stream, animals grazing and kids enjoying the swimming holes. Homes of the day in this area had only dirt floors

42 **Truck Transport**

Plantation field workers like these in Pepeʻekeo in the 1940s were loaded and unloaded at designated gathering points. The mills blew large whistles that signaled the end of the workday, but when lights were added to field machinery, harvests by machine often continued far into the night. *North Hawaiʻi Community Federal Credit Union*

42 **Pepeekeo Mill Camp Gym**
Although the gym at Pepeekeo Mill Camp is now gone, the old mill by the seacliff still stands. The gym
was often used for community gatherings and celebrations, while the camp also had a Japanese clubhouse,
a restaurant, a movie theater and a Catholic church. Here schoolgirls in the 1950s perform the *tinikling*
folk dance of the Philippines. The dancers pranced rhythmically in and out of a pair of snapping bamboo poles.
It was exciting and a bit risky, and dancers were applauded for their skill and courage. *Cabatu Family Collection*

42 May Day 1929

Pepeekeo School served students from Kawainui, Pepeekeo Mill Camp, Andrade Camp, Makahanaloa (Maukaloa), Kaupakauea and Onomea. The former school grounds are now the site of the Pepeʻekeo Community Center.
The few students who progressed beyond the eighth grade attended Hilo Intermediate School, then Hilo High.
Here the third grade boys perform a May Dance at the school's 1929 May Day celebration, which also includes a May Queen and a maypole. Until the 1960s, as elsewhere in the Islands, Hāmākua Coast kids could go to school barefoot.

Okimoto Family Collection

42 **Pepeekeo Train Station**

This depot stood in the Kawainui section of Pepeʻekeo, on the *makai* side of the four-mile Scenic Route. Today a roadside snack shop stands just across the road from the site. Here in 1946, William Moniz poses after posting a number on the building to prepare it for auction, following the closing of the Hawaii Consolidated Railway. The photo was taken by John O. May, a high school student whose father was a railway inspector.

John O. May Collection/Laupāhoehoe Train Museum

44 Mule Wagon

Alia Figueroa hauls kerosene and firewood with Yoshitaka Mikami in 1930, a time of transition from animal to mechanical power. A new gym is under construction behind them in Onomea Camp. Plantation supervisors lived in the homes on the hill. In the 19th Century, writer Mark Twain is said to have visited Onomea, perhaps staying somewhere on this same hill. This "downtown" area had two stores, a stable, a clinic, a bus garage and a Japanese language school. All of it was planted over with cane fields in the 1970s. *Okimoto Family Collection*

Camp Life in Onomea

In the late 1800s Onomea's sugar mill was powered by diverted stream water delivered by flumes. The sophisticated machinery that made this possible was imported from Scotland, landed at Onomea Bay and hauled up to the mill by mules. The mill was dismantled by the 1920s, after operations were transferred to Pāpa'ikou.

In the 1930s Hāmākua Coast plantations provided both homes and family garden spaces to their workers, who grew vegetables from their homelands in these small plots. Portuguese sweetbread was shared with the community during Catholic Holy Ghost Festivals. Japanese workers passed out sweet *mochi* rice cakes at New Year's. Summer *bon* dances were staged by Japanese Buddhists with visitors who came from as far away as Hilo. Camp residents and their friends provided the singing and drumming for these dances.

Kids in the area walked to Pepeekeo School each weekday, unless they could sneak a ride on the train. This walk was often taken in the rain, but they could enjoy eating sweet guavas and chewing sugar cane along the way. Upon returning from school in the afternoon, Japanese children usually attended an hour at Onomea Nipponjin Gakko, the Japanese language school, with its heavy emphasis on traditional Japanese values such as honesty, perseverance, character, respect for elders and filial piety. Saturday mornings brought exams, school cleanup and more cultural lessons. Boys learned the fencing martial art of *kendo*, while girls learned Japanese sewing.

Onomea Camp in the 1930s was a small, tight-knit community. Doors were left unlocked. Neighbors watched each other's kids. Girls played jump rope, bean bag, jacks, master and dolls. Boys played marbles and rolled auto tires. Softball could be enjoyed in the mule pasture, once the mule was chased away.

Camp life was a shared community, with a strong paternal plantation providing local government services and an isolated view of the outside world. Life changed with increasing political and economic benefits, but this was coupled with an increasing need for self-reliance and personal responsibility. The children grew up, were educated and moved out. The camps aged. But while residents saw the need to modernize, they continued to nurture their community values.

43 Summer Hoehana Gang

Hoehana referred to the grueling work (*hana* in Hawaiian) of digging weeds with a garden hoe. Among those toiling in an Onomea Sugar Company field, ca. 1930, are Shizuo Kashiwagi, Manuel Crivello and Jiro Yamaoka (kneeling). Hats were needed to ward off the hot sun and heavy rains of the Hāmākua Coast. School kids worked at *hoehana* during summer breaks. *Okimoto Family Collection*

44 **Shinto Shrine**

The congregation gathers in front of the Onomea Ishizuchi Jinja Shinto Shrine in 1930. The shrine was built around 1908, and its ornate style was quite impressive in such a remote plantation camp. Sumo wrestling was held on the grounds in 1912. When Hilo's Shinto Shrine was damaged in the 1960 tsunami, the congregation temporarily moved to Onomea. When Onomea Camp was dismantled in the late 1960s, the shrine was moved to Hilo Daijingu, a Shinto temple in Hilo. *Okimoto Family Collection*

Special Occation
Anastacio Palpalatoc and Estaquio Manliguis pose in fancy attire ca. 1930, probably at Onomea Camp. The large wooden homes here boasted wide steps and roomy porches that spanned the length of each housefront. The extra polka dots were added to the photo to help commemorate a special occasion. The Manliguis family was well-known on the Big Island for producing high school basketball coaches whose teams won several Hawai'i state championships.
Okimoto Family Collection

96

43 Onomea Flume Gang

In about 1930, Romaldo Fiesta, Fukutaro Desaki, Isabelo Billedo and Melian Emiliano prepare to bundle cut cane for dropping into a wooden flume near Onomea Camp. Workers were often grouped by specialties pertaining to different phases of cane cultivation and harvesting. Immigrants from the Philippines and Japan often worked together, helping develop the mix of languages, foods, clothing and values that characterized Hawaiʻi's plantation communities.

Okimoto Family Collection

44 Okimoto Bus Service

In the 1920s, plantation laborer Nisazuchi Okimoto bought a small grocery store in Onomea Camp. His wife ran the store while he worked for the plantation. Nisazuchi bought a Model-T Ford to replenish his stock in Hilo. Because such private car ownership was rare on the plantation, he was asked to taxi people. Soon he acquired a "banana wagon" (station wagon), a sampan bus and several school buses. The Okimoto fleet, parked here in front of Onomea Gym in 1940, was one of many small bus companies along the Hāmākua Coast. *Okimoto Family Collection*

44 Onomea Bay

The four-mile Scenic Route passes spectacular Onomea Bay, once the site of a fishing village with a Chinese store, a school, a 19th-Century Catholic church, a Japanese saltwater *furo* bath (*shioburo*) and a warehouse. In the 1920s the cliff sides were cultivated in sugar cane and housed the impressive Onomea high flume. Sailing ships anchored offshore and large rowboats were used to move freight in and out. Remnants of an ancient coastal trail used by Native Hawaiians can still be seen near shore. Most of this area is now the Hawai'i Tropical Botanical Garden.

Hawai'i State Archives

44 Onomea Arch

Seen here from the inlet just to the north of Onomea Bay, the Arch was the bay's best-known feature until it collapsed on April 24, 1956, destroyed by forces of nature. An ancient legend tells of a boy and girl from the fishing village who volunteered to be turned into two treacherous rocks in the bay to stop canoe invaders. During World War II, fear of invasion by Japanese forces prompted the installation of heavy artillery from the New York National Guard several miles inland from Onomea Bay. *Hawai'i State Archives*

ベ、イ、イ、ク 本願寺
御 人 佛慶 讃法要記念
□四ハ年七月三十日

45 Pāpaʻikou Hongwanji

In the late 1940s, the congregation of the Pāpaʻikou Hongwanji Mission celebrates its reopening in this old Shingon Buddhist temple. The mission was moved into these temporary quarters after its own original temple was destroyed by fire, under suspicious circumstances, during World War II. The building is still in use today as a private residence, approximately across the Scenic Route from the old Morigaki Store, now operated as a gift shop. A newer Pāpaʻikou Hongwanji, built in the 1950s, stands today at the Hilo end of the Scenic Route. *Pāpaʻikou Hongwanji Mission*

CHAPTER SEVEN
Pāpaʻikou

Consolidating the Camps

Near the intersection of the four-mile Scenic Route on Old Māmalahoa Highway and Highway 19 at Pāpaʻikou, a remnant of the concrete platform of the Paihaʻaloa train station is still visible at the edge of the lawn. In this area the metal rails of the old Hawaii Consolidated Railroad have been partially covered by highway asphalt. From this intersection, Old Māmalahoa Highway continues in the Hilo direction for approximately a half-mile past a Catholic church, school, gym, post office, credit union and former plantation store.

Today's town of Pāpaʻikou and the old Onomea Camp are closely connected historically. Onomea was a bustling community into the 1960s, long after the Onomea Sugar Company transferred its operations down the Hāmākua Coast to Pāpaʻikou early in the 20th Century. Today, with Onomea Camp dismantled, the Onomea name is still evident in "downtown" Pāpaʻikou on Old Māmalahoa Highway—on the still-handsome office building of the former Onomea Sugar headquarters and across the road at Onomea Federal Credit Union.

In the final decades of the Big Island's sugar industry, Onomea Sugar was combined with plantations at Wainaku, Pepeʻekeo, Honomū, and Hakalau to form the Mauna Kea Sugar Company, with all sugarcane processed at a single mill in Pepeʻekeo. Similarly, by the 1970s, the Pāpaʻikou community had absorbed the former residents from many of the smaller camps nearby, including Onomea.

Pāpaʻikou's plantation was the scene of several ambitious efforts in the harvesting and milling process. Cane leaves were chemically analyzed for nutrient deficiencies at the crop log facility, while out in the fields, a "skyhook" was tested to improve harvest productivity. This was an aerial crane— a large engine and winch suspended over the cane fields on a cable. Because it was cumbersome to move from field to field, however, the skyhook saw only limited use.

45 Kalaniana'ole School

Papaikou School opened in the late 1800s as a one-room schoolhouse. It stood at the site of today's Onomea Federal Credit Union on Old Māmalahoa Highway. The school was later moved to its current site, where this building was erected in 1925. It was renamed Prince Jonah Kūhiō Kalaniana'ole School in honor of the beloved Native Hawaiian who served as Hawai'i's delegate to Congress in the 1920s. At one time, the Pāpa'ikou Hongwanji Mission, its Japanese language school and an independent Japanese school stood at the Honoka'a end of the campus. *Okimoto Family Collection*

45 Cockfighting Arena

Cockfighting, more often referred to as "chicken fight," was a very common event at plantation camps. This arena appears to be one that stood in the northern part of Pāpaʻikou in a separate location from the old Papaikou Gym. The 1930's-era arena easily held several hundred people and vendors, especially on Sundays or days off. Although they were illegal, chicken fights regularly drew large crowds wherever they were held. Fighting cocks were highly prized possessions and great care was taken in their feeding and care. *Hawaiʻi State Archives*

45 **Papaikou Pilgrim Church**

Rev. S. Sagawa poses with his flock at Papaikou Pilgrim Church in 1917. The building still stands today without its steeple, as a private home along Old Māmalahoa Highway. A similar church, the Pāpaʻikou Filipino Evangelical Church, still stands near Kalanianaʻole School. Members of both churches eventually moved to the Hilo Coast United Church of Christ in Honomū. These were two of at least nine Pāpaʻikou sites of worship along Old Māmalahoa Highway, including an ancient Hawaiian *heiau*.

Hilo Coast United Church of Christ

45 Railroad Man

Manual Decoito, the Pāpaʻikou Station's train dispatcher and supervisor in the 1930s, stands in front of his home near the station. Pāpaʻikou had another station at Paihaʻaloa, at the intersection of the old and new highways, where the pedestrian overpass is located today. As the Scenic Route begins on Old Māmalahoa Highway, part of this station's concrete platform can be seen along the edge of the lawn near the path to the overpass. *Laupāhoehoe Train Museum*

45 Pāpaʻikou Train Station
The Pāpaʻikou Train Station stood in the grassy area just *mauka* of Highway 19, across from today's Pinky's store. A movie theater, a photo studio, a saloon, a post office, a union hall, a school, a credit union, churches and a small hospital were all within walking distance. A parallel track branched *makai* to the Pāpaʻikou sugar mill. Brave pedestrians had to time their bridge crossings to avoid being hit by the trains that roared past on the narrow vibrating Kapue Stream Bridge.
Laupāhoehoe Train Museum

御入佛式弘中氏宅出立記念
一九四八年十月三十一日

45 T. Hironaka Store

In 1948, today's Pinky's store was the T. Hironaka Store, a retail landmark next to Kapue Stream Bridge. The railway ran just to the right of this photo and is replaced now by Highway 19. Pāpa'ikou's train station (right) was located *mauka* across the track from the store. A railroad warehouse was diagonally across the intersection, where a concrete wall still stands today along the highway. Here, members of Pāpa'ikou Hongwanji pause for a photo while moving their altar from storage at the store to a temporary temple up the coast in Kalaoa. *Pāpa'ikou Hongwanji Mission*

45 Papaikou Mill

Shown here in the 1930s, Papaikou Mill was built just a few feet above sea level. Now dismantled, it was located at a small bay *makai* of the main highway bridge at Kapue Stream. Hideo Matsunaka and Kanichi Tayama are two of the crew standing at upper right. At lower left, a mill supervisor named Anderson stands with his hand on the railing. Papaikou Mill took over the work of smaller mills at Pauka'a and Onomea and featured an engineering marvel for its day—a water-powered elevator. *Hayashi Family Collection*

47 Honoli'i Gulch

Honoli'i Stream crosses beneath Highway 19 just north of 'Alae Cemetery. The old bridge shown here was probably almost underneath, and slightly *makai*, of today's highway bridge, and was photographed before the first railroad span was built nearby. The beach at left is now a popular local surfing spot. *Hawai'i State Archives*

Chapter Eight
Honoliʻi & Wainaku

The Hilo Gateway

On its approach to Hilo from the north, Highway 19 passes above Honoli'i Stream and its picturesque valley, then 'Alae Cemetery on the *mauka* side of the road. At Wainaku, about a mile further south, the scenic overlook on the *makai* side offers a fine overall perspective of the Big Island's county seat. The large structural remains of Wainaku's sugar mill are also visible in this area, including the concrete overpass where sugar trucks once delivered harvested cane to the mill.

The Wainaku area is one of the older neighborhoods along the Hāmākua Coast, with a mix of elegant, venerable residences and simple plantation houses. It neighbors the Ha'aheo area, where legend has it that Kamehameha the Great once commanded thousands of his subjects to cultivate taro in the fields between a Wainaku hill and Waiala Stream near Honoli'i. When done, he proudly stood on the hill near today's Ha'aheo School and declared the name of the place to be *ha'aheo*, or pride.

The entrance into downtown Hilo is accompanied by the sound of tires rumbling over the metal bridge spanning the Wailuku River, which flows out of the saddle between Mauna Kea and Mauna Loa and into Hilo Bay. One theory on the town's name holds that early Polynesians named it for the bay's crescent shape—*hilo* being Hawaiian for the first night of the new moon. In the early 1900's, the area around the lighthouse was a busy spot, with an adjacent train station and a pier limited in its usefulness by rough water. This corner of downtown Hilo was also the site of a meat processing plant, whose bloody runoff into the bay attracted numerous sharks.

Visitor information on popular visitor attractions such as Rainbow Falls (and its open-air market place) is available in the downtown Hilo area at Wailoa Center, the Mo'oheau Bus Terminal, and at the many gift shops, museums and other attractions around town.

46 Nikai Camp

This Japanese immigrant village called Nikai (Second Level) Camp or Nippon (Japanese) Camp was built in the 1880s. The July 24, 1895, edition of the *Pacific Commercial Advertiser* reported that prior to a July 15 fire that destroyed it, the village encompassed "fifty or sixty thatched houses fashioned from bamboo and cane leaves." It had also been a popular tourist attraction. The camp was rebuilt with lumber, later inhabited by Korean immigrants and eventually razed to make way for cane planting. *Pacific Commercial Advertiser*

48 **Funeral in Wainaku**

Mourners gather on Wainaku Street in front of Wainaku Liquors for the funeral of Yukio Narimatsu. Serving as both a home and a business for the Narimatsu family, the store opened in 1925 and was one of many immigrant retail outlets along Old Māmalahoa Highway. It was located on the *mauka* side of the highway, near the entrance to Haaheo School, and has now been replaced by homes. Until the 1960s, funerals were often held at the deceased's home or church. At about the same time, commuting to bigger stores in Hilo became more convenient and eventually, most of the Hāmākua Coast's family stores were closed.
Narimatsu Family Collection

115

The View from Wainaku

The Scenic Point at Wainaku, *makai* of Highway 19 near Mile 4, provides excellent vistas of land and sea, where humpback whales frolic offshore in winter. But it also offers a long look back in time. Viewing the Hilo bayfront from right to left, imagine a bustling Wainaku Mill, a small pier by the lighthouse, and the now-hidden black sand beach that stretched from the Wailuku River to the Wailoa River, where fishing boats are moored today. Here in the early 1800s, Kamehameha the Great harvested huge trees from the nearby slopes and constructed a fleet of war canoes in preparation for his successful conquest of the other islands in the Hawaiian archipelago. The king's statue now stands near the beach, facing the area where this mighty fleet was built.

Before the large breakwater was completed in 1929, the beach at Hilo was a surfing beach. This new breakwater, however, offered no real barrier to the tsunamis that devastated the bayfront on April 1, 1946, and May 23, 1960. The green "front lawn" of Hilo, from the lighthouse area to the high-rise hotels near Coconut Island, once encompassed blocks and blocks of stores and homes. A pier once stood near the hotels.

South of this Scenic Point, where Highway 19 expands into two lanes, the Wainaku Mill once processed sugar cane at the cliff's edge. Imagine a Hawaii Consolidated Railway train traveling just *makai* of the road, the long flumes leading to the mill and the large cane trucks rolling over the wide concrete bridge above. In the 1990s, this old mill site was transformed into the corporate headquarters of C. Brewer & Company, one of the former plantation giants that had diversified into other businesses as sugar slowly disappeared.

49 **Missing Wailuku Bridge Span**

The 1946 tsunami washed out one of three railway bridge spans at the mouth of the Wailuku River, which flows under the arched Pu'ueo Street Bridge near the legendary lava formation known as Maui's Canoe. The two surviving spans were moved to the newly widened Kolekole Bridge up the coast at Hakalau, to become the frame for the new highway bridge.

Pacific Tsunami Museum

50 Sampan Buses

Sampan buses navigate a downtown Hilo intersection near the lighthouse. The sampans were unique Big Island creations—modified passenger cars with custom-made bench seats along the sides and back, offering a kind of mobile living room. They provided cheap, reliable and sociable commutes for Hāmākua Coast residents, as well as an alternative to big buses for schoolchildren. Passenger ships were—and still are—a common site on Hilo's bayfront.

Nani Pierce Collection/Pacific Tsunami Museum

50 Auto Bus

Also called the Motor Car, this hybrid vehicle was used frequently on the Hawaii Consolidated Railway's Hāmākua run, particular in the railroad's later years—the 1930s and early '40s. The Auto Bus was similar to a highway bus fitted with train wheels, an economical alternative to railcars hitched to big locomotives. These simple vehicles contrasted sharply with the railroad's elegant dining cars, with their table service and printed menus. Here, ca. 1940, Hawaii Consolidated general manager Filler (left) and superintendent May pose at the line's Hilo terminus.

Laupāhoehoe Train Museum

51 The Tsunami of 1946

Centuries ago, Hilo's bayfront was a long black-sand beach of scattered marshes and dunes. As the town grew, commercial establishments and a railway were built along this beach, but on April 1, 1946, the massive tsunami swept away nearly all of the structures. Here, at the Wailuku River (center, near breaking waves), the old rail bridge span has been washed away. It was replaced with a new bridge that allowed large waves to pass through it. Today Highway 19 has replaced the railway.

Pacific Tsunami Museum

Resources

Ancient Hawaiian Civilization, Honolulu: Mutual Publishing, 1999.

Bird, Isabella L., *Six Months in the Sandwich Islands*, Honolulu: Mutual Publishing, 1998.

Data Book 1998, Hilo: County of Hawai'i—Department of Research and Development, 1999.

Daws, Gavan, *Shoal of Time*, Honolulu: University of Hawai'i Press, 1968.

Dudley, Walt and Scott C. S. Stone, *The Tsunami of 1946 and 1960 and the Devastation of Hilo Town*, Virginia Beach: The Donning Company, 2000.

Fornander, Abraham, *Ancient History of the Hawaiian People to the Times of Kamehameha I*, Honolulu: Mutual Publishing, 1996.

Hawai'i Tribune Herald, Hilo.

Hilo Tribune Herald, Hilo.

Juvik, Sonia P. and James O. Juvik (ed.), *Atlas of Hawai'i—Third Edition*, Honolulu: University of Hawai'i Press, 1998.

Kalakaua, His Hawaiian Majesty King David, *The Legends and Myths of Hawaii*, Rutland: Charles E. Tuttle Company, 1972.

Kane, Herb Kawainui, *Ancient Hawai'i*, Captain Cook: The Kawainui Press, 1997.

Kurisu, Yasushi "Scotch," *Sugar Town—Hawaii Plantation Days Remembered*, Honolulu: Watermark Publishing, 1995.

Okimoto, Tadao and Atsumu Fujinaka, *Onomea Camp 1935*, Pāpa'ikou, 1982.

Private Landings in Hawaii, 1910.

Pukui, Mary Kawena, *Hawai'i Island Legends—Pikoī, Pele and Others*, Honolulu: Kamehameha Schools Press, 1996.

Pukui, Mary Kawena, Samuel H. Elbert, with Esther T. Mookini and Yu Mapuana Nishizawa, *New Pocket Hawaiian Dictionary*, Honolulu: University of Hawai'i Press, 1992.

Pukui, Mary Kawena, Samuel H. Elbert, and Esther T. Mookini, *Place Names of Hawaii*, Honolulu: University of Hawai'i Press, 1974.

Rogers, Captain Richard W., *Shipwrecks of Hawai'i—A Maritime History of the Big Island*, Hale'iwa: Pilialoha Publishing, 1999.

The Big Island—Electric Century—1894–1994, Hilo: Hawai'i Electric Light Company, 1994.

The Honolulu Advertiser, Honolulu.

The Ready Maphook of East Hawai'i—Year 2001 Edition, Hilo: Odyssey Publishing, 2001.

Index